# TUGBOAT

# TUGBOAT

by Michael Garland

Holiday House / New York

*To my friend Kevin Kearney*

Library of Congress Cataloging-in-Publication Data
Garland, Michael, 1952- author, illustrator.
Tugboat / by Michael Garland. — First edition.
pages cm.
Summary: "A tugboat has many jobs, keeping it busy from morning 'til night. This book shows how
such a little boat can do big jobs. Includes a glossary at the back"— Provided by publisher.
ISBN 978-0-8234-2866-3 (hardcover)
1. Tugboats—Juvenile literature.  I. Title.
VM464.G36 2014
386'.2232—dc22
2012040059

# CONTENTS

The day begins.
The tugboat rests
at the dock.

The captain and
crew board the boat.

The captain steers.
The little boat is ready
to do big jobs.

A cargo ship can cross the ocean,
but it needs a little tug
to help it into port.

A tug can pull a heavy barge
filled with coal or oil.

ENERGY TRANSPORT

A tug can push a beautiful ocean liner with people going on vacation.

And a tug can pull a barge filled
with stinky garbage.
"Hold your nose!"

A tug can carry big parts
for a new bridge.
A tugboat is small, but its engine is strong.

A tug can work
in all kinds of weather.
It can even work
in a snowstorm.

Tugboats pull tall ships.

And on the Fourth of July,
a tugboat pulls the
fireworks barge!

The day ends.
The tugboat rests
at the dock.

**Barge**—A boat that has a flat bottom and carries heavy things.

**Cargo ship**—A ship that carries goods from one part of the world to another.

**Dock**—Where a ship is tied when it is not at sea.

Ocean liner—A ship that carries people.

Port—Where ships can load and unload people or cargo.

Tall ships—Large sailing ships.

Tugboat—A small boat that tows bigger boats and ships.

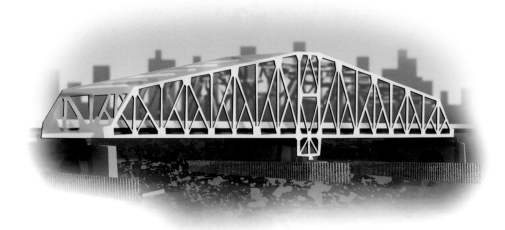

The Willis Avenue Bridge crosses the Harlem River in
New York City. It joins the boroughs of the Bronx and
Manhattan. The bridge was rebuilt in 2011. The center
span of the bridge was built in Albany and placed on
a barge. A tugboat towed the barge down the
Hudson River from Albany to New York City.